Nature's Children

PRAIRIE DOGS

Celia B. Lottridge
and
Susan Horner

GROLIER
EDUCATIONAL

FACTS IN BRIEF

Classification of the Prairie Dog
    Class: *Mammalia* (mammals)
    Order: *Rodentia* (rodents)
    Family: *Sciuridae* (squirrel family)
    Genus: *Cynomys*
    Species: *Cynomys ludovicianus* (includes five subspecies)

World distribution. Exclusive to North America.

Habitat. Open grassy plains.

Distinctive physical characteristics. Brownish fur, lighter underside; short tail and ears; color of tail varies with subspecies.

Habits. Live in large close-knit communities; active only during the day; individuals greet each other by touching muzzles or "kissing."

Diet. Leaves, roots, weeds and grasses.

Published originally as
"Getting to Know . . . Nature's Children."

This series is approved and recommended
by the Federation of Ontario Naturalists.

This library reinforced edition is available exclusively from:

GROLIER
EDUCATIONAL
Sherman Turnpike, Danbury, Connecticut 06816

Contents

Prairie Dogs

Some wild animals live alone, some live with a mate and some live in family groups. But there is one kind of wild animal that lives with hundreds of others in a town. This animal is the Prairie Dog.

Imagine that you are visiting a Prairie Dog town very early on a summer morning. The first thing you would see is a flat, grassy prairie dotted with low mounds of dirt. A closer look at one of these mounds would reveal a hole. This is the entrance to a Prairie Dog's home.

If you watched this entrance carefully you might see a small tan head poke up out of it. But one move from you and the Prairie Dog would disappear back down the hole. It might pop up again though, if you waited very quietly, and maybe even come out for a look around.

Rise and Shine

When the Prairie Dog comes out of its den, you can see that it is about the size of a plump puppy. Not including its tail, it is about 36 centimetres (14 inches) long and covered with thick tan and brown fur that is almost the same color as the dried earth around its home. Its body is plump, and its short tail—10 centimetres (4 inches) long—sticks out behind.

If the Prairie Dog sees nothing to disturb it, it tilts back its head and makes a few short, sharp sounds, or chirks. With each chirk its tail quivers and seems to signal "all clear!"

Soon more Prairie Dogs come out of their homes. They greet each other by kissing and nuzzling. When morning greetings are over, the business of the day begins. The Prairie Dogs feed busily, bask in the sun, take dust baths, visit neighbors or wash themselves.

A new day is underway in the Prairie Dog town.

"All clear!"

Are Prairie Dogs Really Dogs?

There are five kinds of Prairie Dogs in North America. The most common are the Black-tailed and White-tailed Prairie Dogs. Except for the color of their tails, they look very much alike.

The Black-tailed Prairie Dog is found on flat prairies from southern Saskatchewan to Oklahoma and Texas. The White-tailed Prairie Dog lives farther west, in the treeless foothills of Colorado, Utah and New Mexico.

Because their alarm call sounds like the bark of a small dog, early prairie settlers called them Prairie Dogs or prairie barkers. But Prairie Dogs are not really dogs. They are rodents and are related to the mouse, chipmunk, beaver and, most closely, to the Ground Squirrel. Like all rodents they are gnawers. Their teeth are especially good for biting through tough roots and stalks.

From the front it is hard to know which kind of Prairie Dog you are looking at. But the tail will tell you who is who.

Prairie Dog Homes

The hole at the top of a Prairie Dog mound is the entrance to the Prairie Dog's burrow home. The entrance hall is a long tunnel three to four metres (10 to 14 feet) straight down. Then it levels off, continuing deep underground for about the length of a city backyard. Halfway down the entrance tunnel is a shelf where the Prairie Dog can turn around or hide in case of danger.

Small side tunnels lead to sleeping rooms, bathrooms and a larger room where the babies are born. The main tunnel often continues past the bedrooms, joining several burrows together. This way, neighbors can visit without going outside!

The burrow is warm in winter and cool in summer because it is so deep. And it stays dry because the entrance tunnel goes down steeply and then turns up again. Water cannot flow into the tunnels beyond.

Cut-away of a Prairie Dog burrow.

Miniature Mountains

As Prairie Dogs dig their burrows, they push the loose earth out of the tunnel with their foreheads, until there is a pile of dirt at the entrance. They scrape up more earth from around the edges of the pile to make it bigger. Then they butt at the loose heap of dirt with their foreheads and noses until they have shaped it into a firm mound. If you looked carefully at a mound you might see the owner's nose prints.

Prairie Dogs spend a lot of time on their mounds sunning themselves and chatting to each other. Young Prairie Dogs play by climbing up and down these miniature mountains.

These mounds are very important to Prairie Dogs. Because they are higher than the flat land around them they make good lookout posts. By standing on its mound and stretching as tall as possible, a Prairie Dog has a good view all around. The mound also makes a dam to keep any runoff from rain showers from flowing into the burrow entrance.

Opposite page:

This Prairie Dog is hard at work building up its mound.

A Close-knit Community

Prairie Dogs live in groups called coteries. A coterie may start with only one male and one female, but it soon grows to include other adults, some young ones called yearlings and a number of babies. Some coteries have as many as 35 members, but most have fewer than a dozen.

A coterie builds as many burrows and mounds as are needed to hold all of its members. Digging the burrows and keeping them in good repair is a big job, and all the Prairie Dogs in the coterie help with the work. They use their long front claws and short strong legs for digging and their sharp teeth for cutting through roots.

Home on the Range.

Top Dog

The mounds and burrows where a coterie lives and some of the land around them are the territory of that coterie. Visitors are not welcome.

Each coterie is headed by the strongest male. He is the one who comes out of the hole first in the morning and goes in last at night. He knows exactly how much territory belongs to his coterie. If he finds a member of another coterie in his territory he gets to work. He scolds the intruder noisily to scare it off and sometimes even gives the stranger a quick bite on the rump. OUCH!

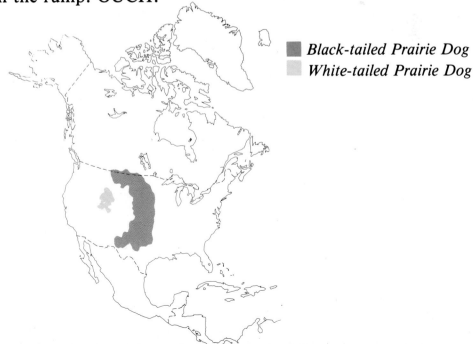

Black-tailed Prairie Dog
White-tailed Prairie Dog

Prairie Dog Town

The territories of many coteries taken together form a Prairie Dog town. Prairie Dog towns, like those people live in, may be large or small. One huge town that existed in Texas many years ago held 400 million Prairie Dogs. It should have been called Prairie Dog City!

Most Prairie Dog towns are much smaller than that, however. Usually they cover about 80 hectares (200 acres) and are home to about 140 coteries or over 1000 Prairie Dogs.

And, like towns people live in, Prairie Dog towns are divided into smaller units, a bit like our blocks. These are called wards and are separated from each other by things such as hills, trees and different kinds of grass.

Prairie Dog village.

Keeping Watch

Every adult Prairie Dog spends some time being a sentinel. While the other Prairie Dogs sun themselves, eat or play, the sentinel sits on its haunches on top of the mound and looks for signs of danger.

If a sentinel sees the shadow of a hawk, hears the yip of a coyote or senses any unusual movement nearby, it sounds the alarm. To do this it rises up on its toes, flicks its tail and barks loudly. Quick as a flash, all the Prairie Dogs dive into their burrows for safety.

For a few moments, all is quiet. Then the sentinel pokes up its head. If the danger has passed, an "all clear" chirk sounds. As quickly as they had disappeared, all the Prairie Dogs pop out of their burrows to resume their busy lives.

At the first sign of danger this alert
Prairie Dog will sound the alarm.

Who Goes There?

Prairie Dogs use touch and smell to recognize the members of their coterie. They know each other very well because they spend a lot of time stroking or grooming each other with their paws. They often groom each other while they sun themselves. They also rub necks and kiss frequently while they are building mounds or looking for food.

Because they know the touch and smell of each other so well they can easily tell friend from stranger. That is why Prairie Dogs greet each other with a kiss. That kiss lets each dog get a good sniff of the other.

Mother and pup greet each other with a kiss.

What's for Dinner?

Prairie Dogs do not have to travel far to find food. They eat the grasses and other leafy plants that grow around their mounds. They choose their favorites by smell and nip the plants off neatly with their sharp teeth. Then they sit up, hold the stem or leaf in their front paws and nibble away. The Prairie Dogs' grassy diet has a useful side effect: all the munching keeps the grass around their mounds well trimmed and gives them a good view over their territory.

Plants also provide Prairie Dogs with the water they need. The stalks of prickly thistles are especially juicy. Prairie Dogs are careful to bite the stalks close to the ground so that they will not get pricked.

In the summer, Prairie Dogs spend more than half of their waking hours eating. It is important for them to eat and get fat while plants are green and plentiful, for in winter food is hard to find.

Opposite page:

Like their relatives the squirrels, Prairie Dogs hold food in their front paws.

Sun Worshippers

Prairie Dogs love warm sunny days. They spend their time waddling about their territory, eating, repairing their mounds, greeting each other with kisses, grooming each other and keeping watch.

If it gets too hot in the middle of the day, they will go into their burrows for a while. Rain, too, will drive them inside. After a rain, though, they love to come out and eat, for the plants are moist and delicious.

Wind makes Prairie Dogs uneasy, probably because the sound of it covers up sounds that might warn them of approaching danger. On windy days they are especially alert and will duck into their holes at any unusual movement.

Fattening up for winter!

A Cozy Retreat

As winter approaches Prairie Dogs concentrate on getting fat. In cold weather, they slow down and spend most of their time in their burrows. But they do not go into a deep sleep and hibernate, as some squirrels do. When the winter weather is fine, Prairie Dogs pop out for a look around and a quick snack on whatever food they can find. However, when winter winds blow, they retreat to the warmth of their underground home.

Prairie Dogs line their bedrooms with dried grasses and weeds.

Mating Time

In early spring, Prairie Dogs become lively again. Food is still hard to find, but they come out of their holes to feel the warmth of the sunshine and greet each other. Soon all the coteries in the town are out. The mounds are abuzz with activity and with the chirking, yipping conversation of Prairie Dogs.

Mating time is March and April. Then, both males and females clean out the old burrows and dig new tunnels. The adult females line the largest sleeping room in the burrow with soft, dry grass to make nests for the babies that will soon be born.

Although young Prairie Dogs are very curious they must be sure to stay close to home.

Prairie Dog Pups

The babies are born in late May. There are usually four or five babies in a litter. They are red, wrinkled, hairless, blind little things about eight centimetres (3 inches) long from nose to tail.

The mother looks after her babies carefully. For the first few weeks she allows no one else near them. She begins to get them ready for a life of grooming and kissing by licking and rubbing them frequently.

The pups grow fast on their mother's rich milk. In three weeks their fur has grown in. Now they can squeak and roll around a little.

At about five weeks they open their eyes. They are starting to look a lot like their parents. Soon they are running around the burrow, trying to bark. And it is not long until the great day when they come out of their holes and tumble down their mounds into the great wide world.

"Pass it on!"

Bringing Up the Babies

Once the pups have come out of their burrows, everyone in the Prairie Dog town helps raise and care for them. The little ones run from one burrow to another to play with the babies from other litters. Sometimes they sleep over at another pup's home. Unlike adult Prairie Dogs, they are even allowed to visit other coteries.

Both male and female adults spend much time grooming the pups, kissing them and playing chasing and tumbling games with them. The pups love these games so much that they sometimes become nuisances. An adult who is trying to keep watch or eat has to discourage them with little nips or pushes.

The babies soon learn to dart into their holes if anything strange happens. They pop in and out of their holes hundreds of times a day like furry little jack-in-the-boxes.

But their babyhood is short. At seven weeks of age, they can find and eat food on their own. At 10 weeks, they are able to look after themselves.

Opposite page:

The tan and brown coat of the Prairie Dog blends in with the soil of the mound.

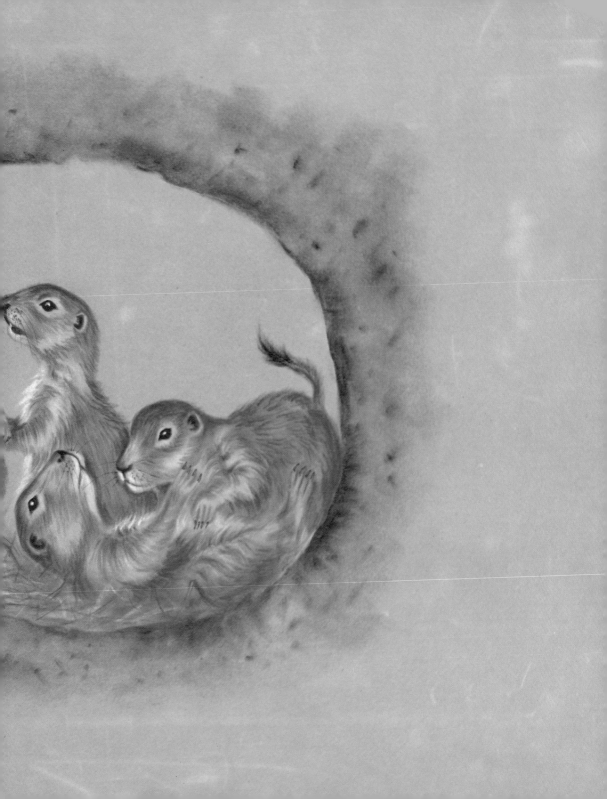

Learning to be Prairie Dogs

Toward summer's end, the spring babies are nearly as big as their parents. Their playing has taught them how to recognize each other, how to groom and "talk" to each other.

Now they begin to learn about territories. They are no longer welcome in the territory of other coteries. They will be driven back to their own territory if they venture far.

They love to copy the older Prairie Dogs. By copying, they learn how to find food, how to respond to alarm calls and how to give calls themselves.

One call the young Prairie Dogs especially like is the territorial call, which seems to mean "Here I am and here is my territory." To give it, the Prairie Dog stands on its hind legs, thrusts its front paws out, raises its nose to the sky and gives a loud two-note bark. The young ones practice this endlessly. Sometimes they get so excited that they lean too far back and tumble over and over, down the mound.

Growing Families

By late summer, the young Prairie Dogs, like the older ones, spend most of their time eating to store fat for the winter. They will spend the winter in the burrow where they were born. In the spring they will be yearlings. Then they will welcome the new litters of babies in the coterie. By the time they are two years old, they will be ready to mate and have babies.

Moving On

A coterie cannot keep growing forever or there will not be enough food for all of its members. So every year some Prairie Dogs have to leave their coteries.

Yearling males sometimes go off to establish coteries of their own. Sometimes an adult male and female may go together and build new burrows and new mounds, leaving the younger members of their original coterie to carry on. Females sometimes leave to join other coteries.

New coteries, new mounds and new burrows will all become part of the Prairie Dog town where Prairie Dogs stand sentinel, work and play together.

Prairie Dogs will only travel as far from their den as they have to when looking for food.

Words to Know

Burrow   A hole in the ground dug by an animal to be used as a home.

Coterie   A group of Prairie Dogs made up of 8 to 35 members.

Litter   Group of animal brothers and sisters born together.

Mating season   The time of year when animals come together to produce young.

Prairie   A flat treeless area where grasses grow.

Pup   Young Prairie Dog.

Rodent   An animal with a certain kind of teeth, which are especially good for gnawing.

Sentinel   A guard that watches for danger and signals alarm if necessary.

Territory   Area that an animal or group of animals lives in and often defends from other animals of the same kind.

Ward   Sub-division of a Prairie Dog town.

Yearling   Animal that is one year old.

INDEX

Cover Photo: Barry Ranford

Photo Credits: Dennis Schmidt (Valan Photos), pages 4, 26; Brian Milne (First Light Associated Photographers), pages 7, 12; Stephen J. Krasemann (Valan Photos), pages 8, 25, 33, 34, 37, 43; Esther Schmidt (Valan Photos), pages 15, 21, 40; Robert C. Simpson (Valan Photos), page 16; Wayne Lankinen (Valan Photos), pages 18-19, 29, 30, 46; Wilf Schurig (Valan Photos), page 22; Thomas Kitchin (Valan Photos), page 44.

Printed and Bound in Italy by Lego SpA